Laughables

A Humorous Look at the Pressures, Predicaments, and Pleasures of Being a Woman

By The Jantz and Bickel Families

HARVEST HOUSE PUBLISHERS
Eugene, Oregon 97402

Copyright © 1984 by Harvest House Publishers
Eugene, Oregon 97402

Library of Congress Catalog Card Number 83-82320
ISBN 0-89081-401-5

All rights reserved. No portion of this book may be reproduced in any form without the written permission of the Publisher.

Printed in the United States of America.

Dedication

This book is dedicated to four special Christian women—
our mothers:

Erna, the energetic;
Evie, the effervescent;
Jo, the jubilant; and
Loyce, the lint-loather.

Life with them was just crazy enough
to give us a humorous outlook on life's ordinary experiences.

Contents

INTRODUCTION

1. **CHILDREN**
   *Enduring the Ordeal From
   Diapers To Diplomas* 11

2. **FRIENDS AND RELATIVES**
   *Relationships Which May Be
   Hazardous To Your Health* 33

3. **ROMANCE**
   *Riding the Roller Coaster
   Of Love* 59

4. ***WORKING***
   At Home, At the Office,
   And In Other Disaster Zones 83

5. ***GROWING OLDER GRACEFULLY***
   Can You Fool All of the People
   All of the Time? 105

Introduction

It's difficult to imagine anyone with an existence more dull than ours. We're two very typical suburban families who for some reason have landed smack dab in the middle of average. We're so typical, George Gallup could use us for the median range on any poll and never be wrong. Not that we mind. We love being this way, even if it does seem unexciting. If someone made a bumper sticker which read, "Mediocre is Marvelous," we would be the first to buy it.

We each have a girl and a boy and two Strolee car seats. Neither of us can afford our house payments, but that's all right; we can't afford our utilities either.

Because of this propensity for the mundane, we didn't think we had much to contribute to the current genre of popular literature, which seems to thrive on the spectacular.

On the other hand, there are a lot of you out there who are just as dull as we are—maybe even more so! Perhaps you will agree that it is time for a lighthearted book about the adventures of the average life.

This book focuses on life's ordinary experiences: family, friends, church, responsibilities. In reality, these things are very special. We treasure the many rewards which come from the common circumstances God has given to us.

The little stories in this book demonstrate that while the average life is not always glamorous, it can bring blessings, giggles, and a few guffaws.

Cheryl & Bruce Bickel
Karin & Stan Jantz
Fresno, California

1

CHILDREN
Enduring the Ordeal From Diapers To Diplomas

Children

    Children are a gift from God. The miracle of birth is an amazing fact. You may have your own children, or you may fulfill the special role of grandmother, aunt or "big sister." Whatever the relationship, you recognize the special worth of children.

    There are times, however, when a child's behavior may lead you to suspect that either all of God's creations are not perfect, or that God is a practical joker. Consequently, you may have the fiendishly fleeting thought of embroidering your child's lips together. Or, maybe you have contemplated muffling the boisterous voices of the neighborhood children by cramming their skateboards down their throats.

    Here are a few examples of the trials and tribulations in which children delight and from which you take flight.

CHILDREN

The Hectic Life

Peace, tranquility, and privacy. These seem like inalienable rights. But true solitude is an impossibility if you have children between the ages of 2 and 19 years old. The mother with children living at home dreams of retreating to the solitary life in the Gobi Desert or in a guru's cave in the Himalayan Alps.

Her day does not begin with the sweet and placid chirpping of a robin outside her window. Instead, she is awakened by someone yelling from the laundry room for a pair of clean underwear. She must immediately rush to the kitchen where she has to act as cook/waitress/busboy at breakfast, to make bag lunches, and to scrub the chocolate milk stain out of the glass which somebody didn't rinse out the night before.

At the same time she has to serve as referee between two children fighting over the twirling plastic toy that came out of the cereal box. In the midst of all this, she must get dressed and try to comb her hair

CHILDREN

by looking at her reflection in the shiny part of the refrigerator door handle.

With the skill of a military strategist, she schedules her day to coordinate the car pool, grocery shopping, an appointment at the pediatrician, and returning home to meet the repairman who will fix the garbage disposal that choked on the twirling plastic toy that she threw in it this morning. She actually manages to get some free time from 11:32-11:37 A.M., but this is disrupted when her husband calls and asks: "If you aren't too busy, could you stop by three or four hardware stores and see who has the best price on barbecue tongs?"

After returning from her part-time job at the complaint department of a used car lot, the rest of her day is spent in a blur of dusting, darning, dinner, and dishes. It seems like one child is continually clamped to her left calf, and there are simultaneous screams for her assistance

CHILDREN

from opposite ends of the house. Her day has been a constant chain of catastrophes.

Finally, she can endure it no longer. In exasperation and desperation, she bellows a demand to be left alone for a few minutes, and she beats a hasty withdrawal for seclusion.

After barricading herself in the bathroom, she finds a moment of solitude and peace. She sinks to the floor, revelling in this moment in time which is free from interruptions. Then, as she is gently massaging her bunions, she sees a little piece of paper wiggling its way under the door. She tries to ignore it, but she is overcome with curiosity. On the paper is scribbled a note which reads: "We are sorry to bother you. But we were just wondering, what's the phone number for the fire department?"

CHILDREN

First Day of School

On your child's first day of school, you must prepare yourself psychologically. As you walk up the sidewalk holding his sticky hand, he thinks you will never leave his side. He thinks you will be there to caress him when he splinters his skull with his toy hammer. He thinks you will be there to comfort him when he gets a crayon stuck in his ear. In his ignorant bliss, he is eager to start school.

You leave him on the playground and resist the urge to kiss his cowlick into place. Instead, you wipe his nose and give his jacket zipper a symbolic tug all the way to the top to protect him from the wind and all other evils to which he will be exposed without you.

As you walk away, you hear him whimper. Maybe he **does** realize what is happening. You don't want him to be distraught, but you feel better now that he is crying his heart out.

CHILDREN

You take a quick glance over your shoulder. He is being consoled by his new teacher. You know that your son will consider her a weak substitute in place of your love. Then the teacher waves at you and says, "He's all right. You just caught his Adam's apple in the zipper."

CHILDREN

Car Trips

There will probably be a special jewel in the heavenly crown of every woman who has committed the supreme act of love and self-sacrifice—taking a long car trip with young children.

It begins when Daddy volunteers to drive. He is no fool. He knows that if his hands are on the wheel, Mommy will have to spend most of the three-hour trip to Grandma's house performing "automobile acrobatics" over the front seat to attend to children in the back seat.

At times she feels like a circus contortionist as she simultaneously:
- pulls the lollipop out of Jeffrey's nostril;
- retrieves a pencil off the floor; and
- uses a wadded Kleenex to sop up a bottleful of milk which has spilled on the back seat.

But the worst aspect of the trip is her husband. As she turns backward

CHILDREN

over the front seat to attend to some childhood calamity, he begins to pat her bottom like a set of bongo drums, singing a calypso tune in the process.

Then he makes some snide remark about how he can't see the traffic behind him because her well-padded rear end is blocking his view in the mirror. Maybe that is why they call it a "rear" view mirror.

CHILDREN

Billy's First Job

A kid's first job can be a traumatic experience—for Mom.

There's something about seeing your son or daughter go to work for the first time which produces mixed emotions of fear, insecurity, and pride.

"You're finally making something of yourself, Billy. Your father and I are very proud."

"Aw, Mom, I'm only clearing tables at Mr. Burger. It's no big deal."

"I know, but you look so grown-up in that little paper hat shaped like a sesame seed bun."

"I've got to go, Mom. I'll be late for work."

"This is it, I suppose. Be sure to write."

"I'm only working six and a half hours a week. It's not like I'm going off to the Big Apple or something."

"Just the same, call me when you get there. It's a jungle out there,

CHILDREN

Billy. Are you sure you don't want me to drive you?"

"Mom, I can walk, remember? Mr. Burger is just around the corner. I'll see you."

"Bye, Billy! Do well! I'll pray for you! And don't get any mustard stains on your polyester uniform."

"Bye, Mom."

CHILDREN

Blessings on all who reverence and trust the Lord—on all who obey him!

Their reward shall be prosperity and happiness. Your wife shall be contented in your home. And look at all those children! There they sit around the dinner table as vigorous and healthy as young olive trees. That is God's reward to those who reverence and trust him.

May the Lord continually bless you with heaven's blessings as well as with human joys.

May you live to enjoy your grandchildren! And may God bless Israel!

Psalm 128

CHILDREN

Family Vacation

The best time to take a family vacation is before the kids scatter. As soon as your oldest daughter's acne starts to clear up, she'll be off to college. Your high-school-aged son may finally get the summer job he's always dreamed about: cleaning the noses of the presidents on Mt. Rushmore. And your 10-year-old daughter may soon be living in a halfway house for video game addicts.

You suggest a serene weekend at the mountain cabin where the family can spend some quality time together. Your kids want to go to Disneyland for some family "action" and "excitement." (Translation: They want to go someplace where they can ditch you and be on their own.)

The Disneyland vacation turns out to be one of those motherhood experiences you will never forget—like labor pains. Your older daughter refuses to enjoy herself and describes everything as

CHILDREN

"juvenile." Your son spends his time ignoring your instructions while he gawks at the girls. And your younger daughter is so obnoxious that you want to throw her overboard on the African Jungle Cruise ride.

The only time you actually spend with the family is when you are waiting in long, crowded lines. It is hard to foster family togetherness when you are surrounded by masses of humanity all dressed in bermuda shorts.

Your family members become even more alienated back at the hotel. Your older daughter won't speak to anyone. Your younger daughter told the cute bellboy that your older daughter wears pimple cream. And your son flushed your souvenir Mousketeer ears down the toilet.

So much for the Disneyland vacation. Next year everyone can spend a weekend at the mountain cabin. But to preserve family unity, each family member will have to go on a different weekend.

CHILDREN

Children are a gift from God; they are his reward. Children born to a young man are like sharp arrows to defend him. Happy is the man who has his quiver full of them...
                                                            Psalm 127:3-5

CHILDREN

You Know You Are A Mother When:

★ Your son comes home from college and has rented a U-Haul trailer to carry the dirty clothes he wants you to wash.

★ You have an assortment of 17 handmade clay ashtrays and no one in your family smokes.

★ Your 3-year-old child calls you into the bathroom to retrieve the Star Wars soldier out of the toilet.

★ Your freezer is packed with the 27 boxes of Girl Scout cookies your daughter couldn't sell to anybody else.

★ You are in a clothes store and your teenage daughter keeps calling you by your first name so nobody will suspect that she is shopping with her mom.

★ You catch yourself singing the theme song from the "Mr. Rogers' Neighborhood" show.

2

FRIENDS AND RELATIVES
Relationships Which May Be Hazardous To Your Health

Friends And Relatives

Relationships with family and friends can be filled with blessings, but they can offer occasional booby traps as well. You must approach such relationships with a degree of caution. For example:

★ When your friend is complimenting your cooking, she may be setting you up to cater the next P.T.A. banquet.

★ If your sister-in-law asks for a few sewing pointers, you may end up making all the uniforms for her Girl Scout troop.

★ And then there's your mother. She was so proud of your portrayal of a rock in your second-grade class play. Now she is telling the pastor that you should be in charge of the church's Christmas pageant because of your prior experience.

FRIENDS AND RELATIVES

The following highlights are just a few more examples of how these seemingly harmless relationships may exhaust your energies and sap your sanity.

A mirror reflects a man's face, but what he is really like is shown by the kind of friends he chooses.

Proverbs 28:19

FRIENDS AND RELATIVES

Long Time No See

It's a hot summer day. You're washing the morning dishes as the kids are screaming in the family room. You try to keep one eye on the bran muffins baking in the oven while watching television with the other. Phil Donahue is discussing the merits of admitting perverts into the priesthood.

Suddenly the door bell chimes. You head for the door, tripping over two Tonka trucks and a Barbie doll. You manage to kick enough debris aside to get the front door open.

There stands Libby. Libby was your intellectual girl friend from college. Libby with the round horn-rimmed glasses, the khaki skirt, and penny loafers. The glasses are the same, but the $400 suit and leather briefcase are new. So is the Mercedes parked in front.

"Libby, how good to see you again," you intone. "Come in, please come in." By now your kids have rushed over, grabbed you

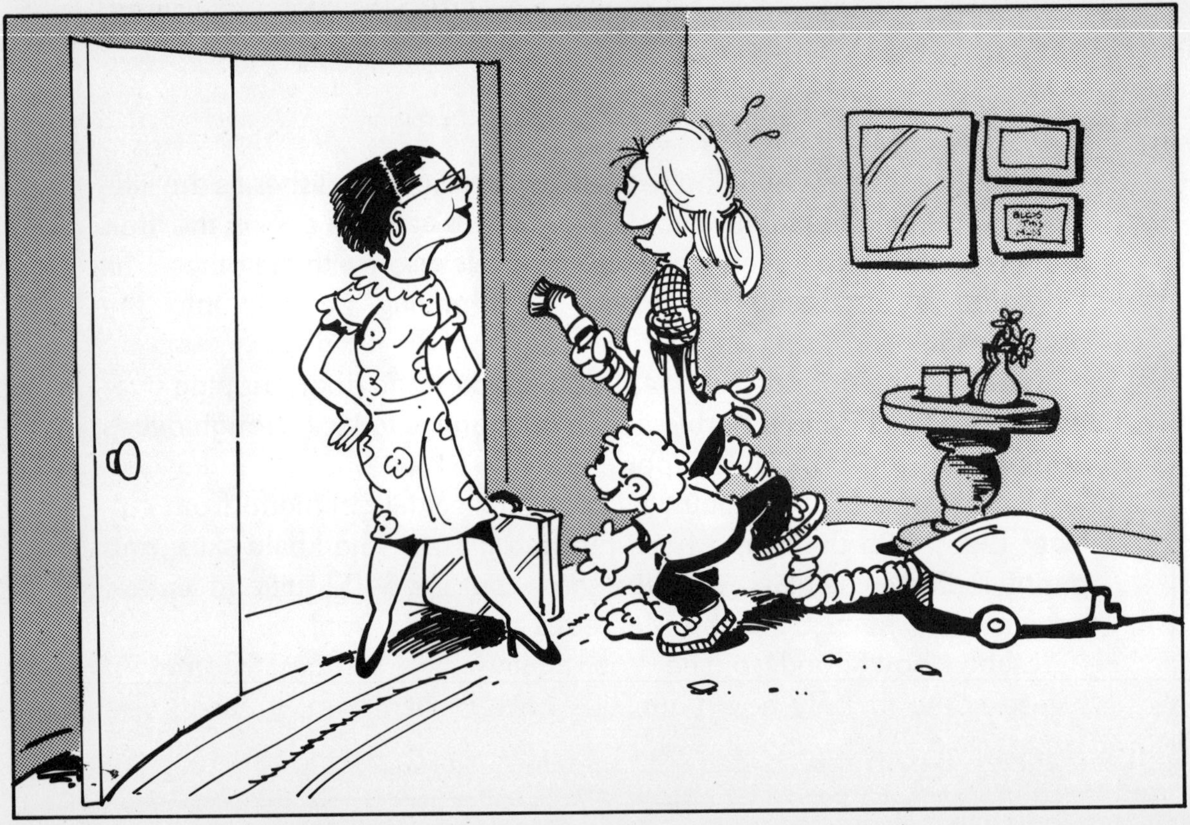

FRIENDS AND RELATIVES

by the legs, and are yelling, "Who's that?"

You lead Libby into the living room, where you have to move a pile of dirty laundry so the two of you can sit down and talk over old times. Your reunion lasts only 45 minutes, but it is enough time for you to relax and reflect on those memorable college days.

You say good-bye with a feeling of self-worth, having engaged in an intelligent conversation for the first time in years. That is, until you reach up to brush back your bangs and feel the Strawberry Shortcake clippies you borrowed from your daughter to keep your hair back while you were washing dishes. Then you notice your wrinkled T-shirt and frayed cutoffs, and from the kitchen you detect the distinct odor of burnt bran muffins.

FRIENDS AND RELATIVES

A friendly discussion is as stimulating as the sparks that fly when iron strikes iron.

Proverbs 27:17

FRIENDS AND RELATIVES

Gift-Giving

If you are running out of storage space in the garage and attic, it is probably the fault of your friends and relatives. Not all of your friends and relatives. Just the ones whose gifts you open in the bathroom with the shower water running full blast so no one will hear you laughing. It's not that you don't appreciate the thought. It's just that you don't appreciate the gift.

The gifts you get from Cousin Mildred are a good example. Many people think that homemade gifts are the best. They think this until they get one from Cousin Mildred. Her specialty is little cupid statuettes molded out of the excess wax build-up from her floors.

Let's not forget your brother Derrell, the family prankster. No longer does he give Ex-Lax disguised as chocolate candy. He has graduated to more fiendish treats like a full-page newspaper ad congratulating you on your 41st birthday (when you are only 37). Or more sadistic gifts,

FRIENDS AND RELATIVES

like a bathroom scale that always registers seven and a half pounds more than you weigh.

Then there is your wealthy friend Daisy. She is the one who puts mimeographed lists of gift ideas in the neighborhood mailboxes the week before her birthday. When it's your birthday, however, she sends a used birthday card which she bought at a garage sale. She glues a dime inside the card and writes: "Go get a soda."

From your neighbor Lois, you get a pot holder she made on her loom. In all the years that you've known her, on every occasion she gives you a pot holder. You now have enough pot holders to insulate your attic. But still they keep coming. Pot holders are the only thing Lois knows how to make on her loom.

Over the years you have refused to discard these gifts or to send them to the Ripley's Believe It Or Not Museum. Instead, you keep them in your garage because someday you may be able to give them to

FRIENDS AND RELATIVES

somebody else as a birthday or wedding gift. Some newlywed couple may really enjoy a 3-foot-high, plaster-of-Paris statue with a glow-in-the-dark belly button which plays the theme song from "The Dukes of Hazzard."

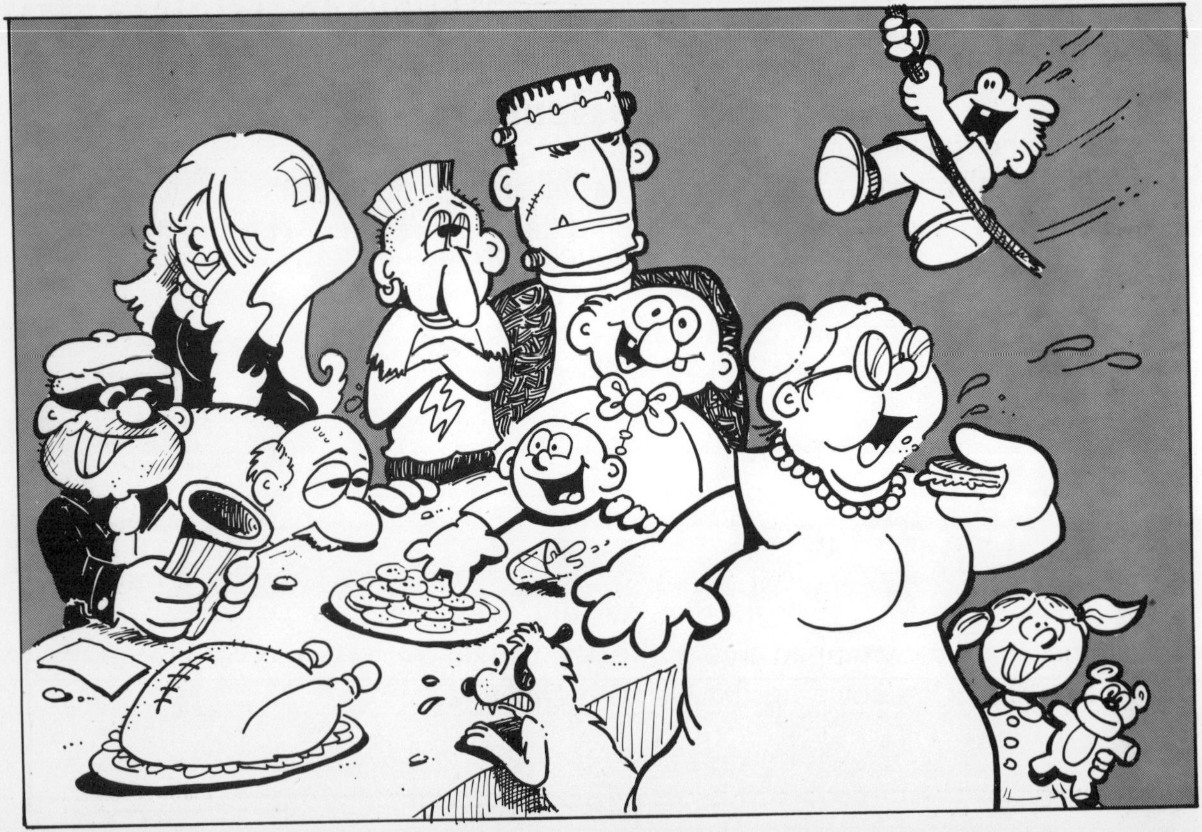

FRIENDS AND RELATIVES

Family Reunion

When it is time for the family reunion, a very strange assortment of humans and sub-humans shows up at your doorstep. A quick glance convinces you that they have emerged from dark closets, underneath rocks, and from a home for the criminally insane. Your own family is bad enough, but then come the in-laws and the friends of the in-laws.

Fortunately, this group of strange relations only comes to your home every few years or so—otherwise you would surely be discovered by the camera crew of "That's Incredible." You recognize about half of them. The other half remind you of the figures in the Ripley's Believe It Or Not Museum.

For instance, standing within striking distance of the condiment tray is Aunt Iris. She once sneaked into the refrigerator on Thanksgiving and licked the whipped cream off the pumpkin pie. (The next year you tricked her by covering the pie with Noxema.)

FRIENDS AND RELATIVES

Your husband's nephew always shows up with a cheap-looking blonde. Then there's that polite young man who is admiring your antique vase collection. It happens that he is your cousin's brother-in-law and is out on parole for petty theft.

And let's not forget little Timmy—the boy who was born with suction cups instead of hands and feet. His favorite pastime is climbing bookcases and dropping pimiento olives down the necklines of ladies' dresses.

But perhaps the strangest phenomenon from this entire wonderland of the weird occurs when everyone leaves. Each person goes away convinced that he or she is the only normal one in the entire family.

FRIENDS AND RELATIVES

The remarkable thing about family pride is that so many people can be so proud of so little.

FRIENDS AND RELATIVES

The Favored Son/Daughter

The favored son/daughter phenomenon exists in nearly every family where two or more siblings are present. This is the situation in which parents choose a child from among their litter and silently declare him to be their favorite.

The choosing must be done silently, because no self-respecting parent would openly tell a child in the presence of other brothers or sisters that he is more favored. Joseph with his multicolored coat was a victim of open favoritism in the Old Testament, and it got him thrown into a pit. Not a nice way to spend your summer vacation.

Usually parents will pick out the child who hasn't made much of himself and make him the favored one. No one knows why this is, except that the good-for-nothing needs all the help he can get. It's a strange sight to watch. An example is when all the kids in the family bring home school projects.

FRIENDS AND RELATIVES

Billy makes a nuclear rocket launcher in his fifth-grade science class, and all he gets is a "That's nice, Billy." Susan paints a striking replica of the Mona Lisa with a Crayola watercolor set and hears the comment, "Why isn't the lady in the picture smiling?"

But when Marvin, the favored son, brings home his ant farm project in a grocery sack, the parents respond by saying things like, "What a remarkable scientific achievement" or "Such attention to detail," while Marvin wolfs down two Twinkies on the sofa.

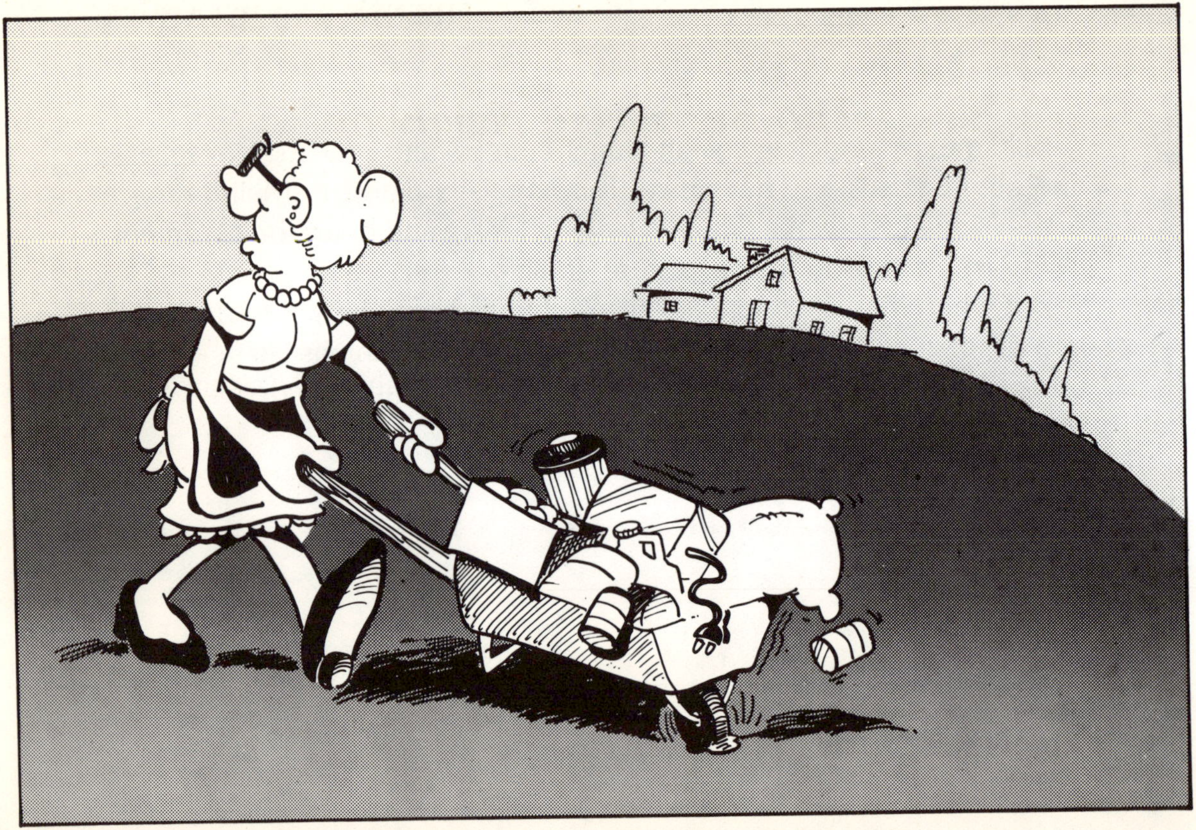

FRIENDS AND RELATIVES

The Borrowing Neighbor

In order to protect your God-given worldly possessions, you must beware of the neighbor who seeks to borrow them. It starts innocently with borrowing a cup of sugar. But if not held under control, it can escalate to borrowing your Thanksgiving turkey and dressing—and all you get back is a carcass of bare bones and a dirty Tupperware container.

As you build resistance to your neighbor's requests, you must then learn to detect the more devious approaches. For example, there is the old "Injured Child Phone Call" ploy. This is where your neighbor calls and frantically cries: "Billy has been hurt and is bleeding very badly. Could you please rush over with some Band-Aids and a loaf of bread?"

If your neighbor has been thwarted often enough, she may stoop to the "Scavenger Hunt" scam. In this scheme, your neighbor comes to your door with several friends or family members. She announces that

FRIENDS AND RELATIVES

you are the last stop on a scavenger hunt, and her team needs only one more item to win. Could you possibly give her any *one* of the following items?

1. A hair from the head of Herbert Hoover;
2. A $4 bill;
3. The eye of a newt; or
4. Two pounds of hamburger meat.

Don't be fooled by this charade to confiscate your hamburger meat. Call her bluff and give her that hair from the head of Herbert Hoover which you have been saving.

FRIENDS AND RELATIVES

*Just as the rich rule the poor,
so the borrower is servant to the lender.*
                                                    Proverbs 22:7

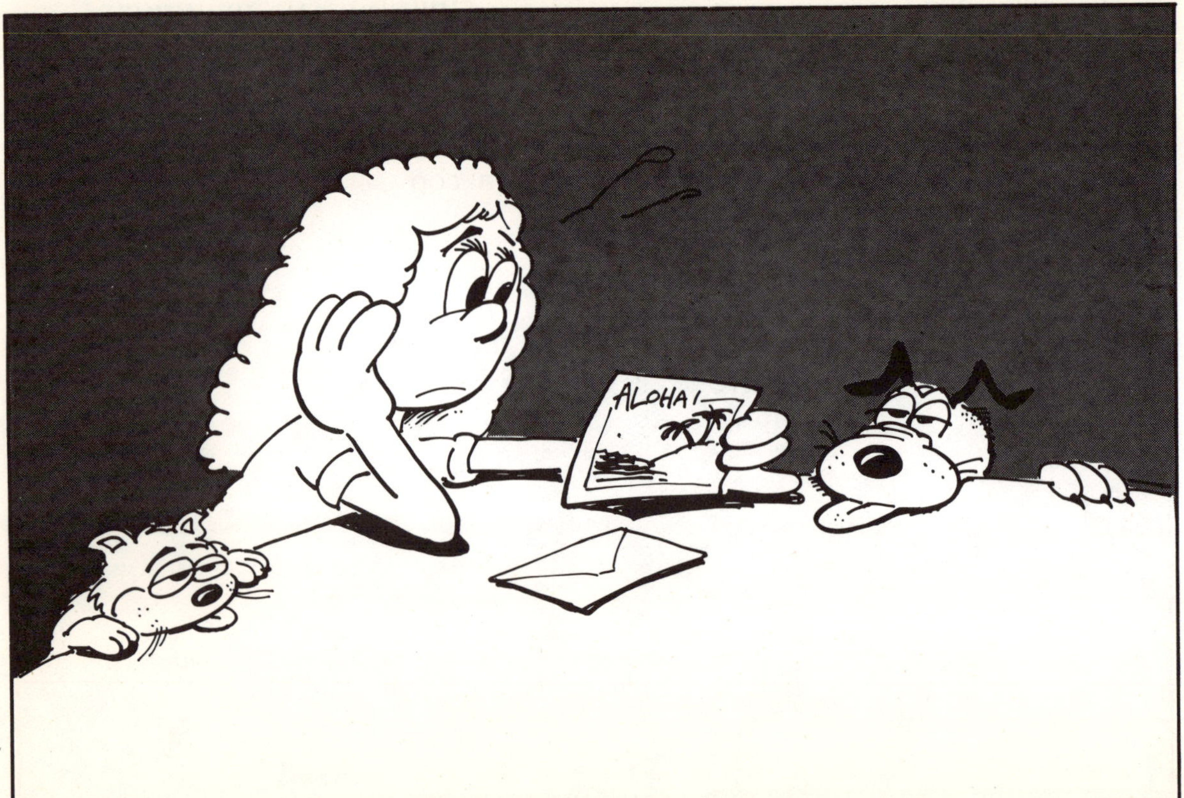
ALOHA!

FRIENDS AND RELATIVES

You Know You Need a Friend When:

★ Someone anonymously sends you a copy of a book entitled *I'm Okay, You're So-So.*

★ You have just finished hosting a ladies' luncheon for the new pastor's wife. After all the guests have gone, you walk by your hall mirror and notice that the back of your dress is unzipped.

★ Your relatives send you a postcard from their vacation in Hawaii which reads: "Weather is here. Wish you were beautiful."

★ You are moving to a new house and all the friends who volunteered to help you are now "mysteriously" out of town for the weekend, occupied with some family emergency, or suffering from a sudden bout of the flu.

★ A get-well card from your Sunday school class reads: "Our

FRIENDS AND RELATIVES

class wishes you a speedy recovery (by a vote of 7 to 5)."

★ Stepping from the store dressing room, you ask your shopping companion how you look in a new outfit, and she replies: "Some questions are better left unanswered."

A true friend is always loyal,
and a brother is born to help in time of need.
Proverbs 17:17

FRIENDS AND RELATIVES

There is a saying, 'Love your friends and hate your enemies.' But I say: Love your enemies! Pray for those who persecute you! In that way you will be acting as true sons of your Father in heaven. For he gives his sunlight to both the evil and the good, and sends rain on the just and on the unjust too. If you love only those who love you, what good is that? Even scoundrels do that much. If you are friendly only to your friends, how are you different from anyone else? Even the heathen do that.

Matthew 5:43-47

3

ROMANCE
Riding the Roller Coaster Of Love

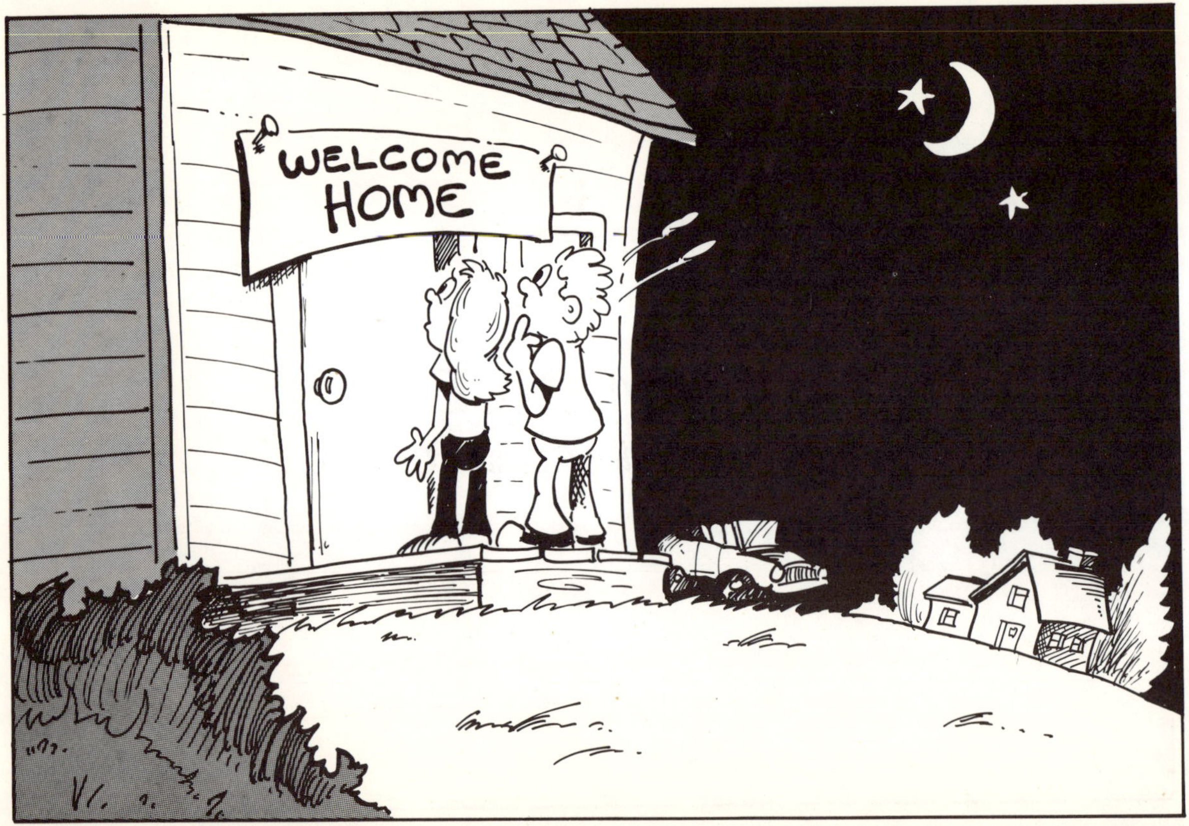
WELCOME HOME

Romance

    As a young girl, you used to daydream of spending a lifetime of living "happily ever after" with your handsome prince. Being older and wiser, you realize there are times when romance seems to have vanished and a wicked witch has turned him into a castle gargoyle. This can happen whether your prince is your husband, fiance, steady beau, or just an innocent victim you're trying to snare. Let's face it—there are times when he seems oblivious to romance and acts like a toad.

    You realize, of course, that romance is not a necessity of life, but like a roller coaster: You could live without it, but it does add fun and excitement to your life. Unfortunately, along the way there are some sharp dips that make your stomach drop to your knees. For instance,

ROMANCE

how about when his idea of a romantic interlude is sharing a bowl of potato chips with you while watching Monday Night Football highlights? But that is just one of the swerves on the roller coaster. Here are a few others.

ROMANCE

The Singles Group

The unmarried Christian woman may occasionally find herself in a "singles group." This is a place where she is supposedly given the opportunity to meet an unattached male. However, she must learn to quickly spot and avoid some bachelors who usually fall into one of three categories:

1. ***The "Vinnie" Type.*** He wears his shirts a size too small so his shoulders will look bigger. He has a punk rock sticker on his car windshield, and he calls women "chicks." He thinks it looks macho to spit and walk with a limp.

2. ***The "Dirk" Type.*** Here is a man who dresses well and has a nice job. He is good looking and is a fine conversationalist. Your first impression is that he is a great guy. Unfortunately, he has that same impression of himself. In restaurants, he likes to sit near the window so he can see his own reflection.

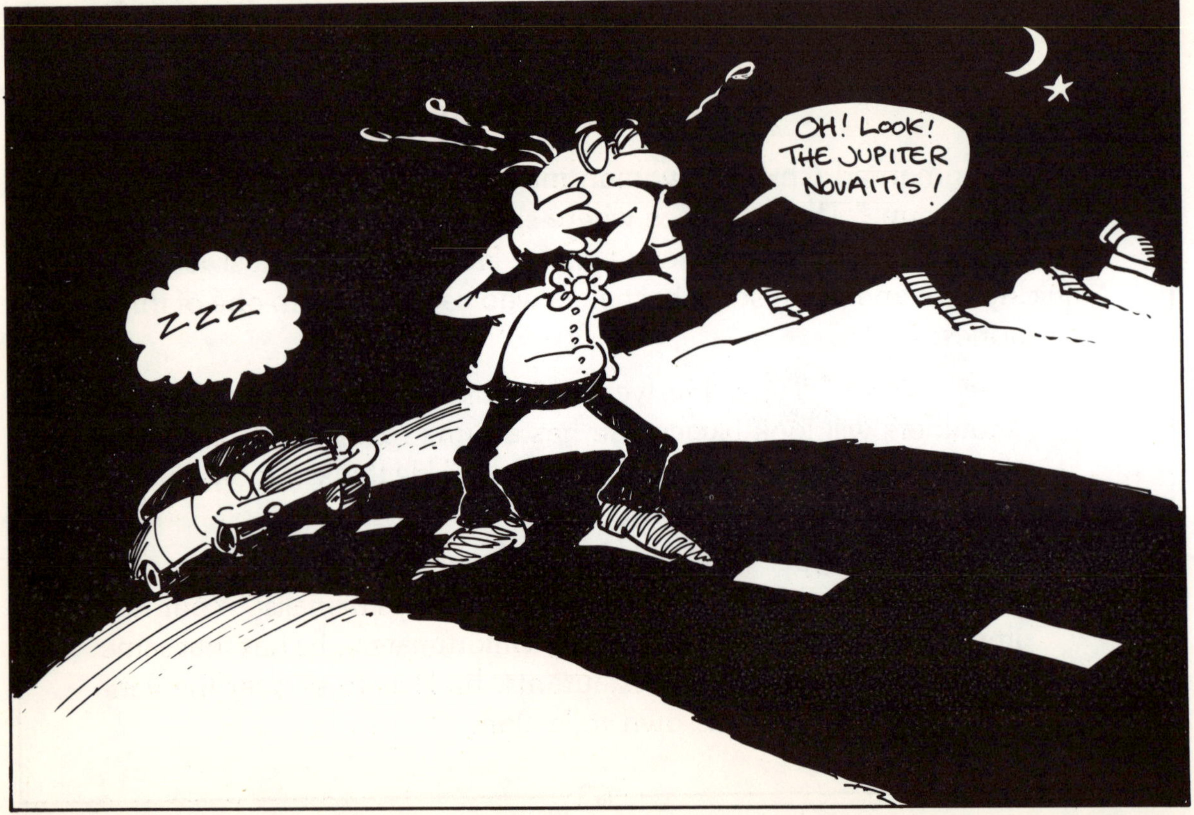
ZZZ
OH! LOOK! THE JUPITER NOVAITIS!

ROMANCE

3. ***The "Harold" Type.*** This guy is a computer programmer who looks like Ichabod Crane with wire-rimmed glasses. He carries a plastic pocket liner filled with fountain pens and mechanical pencils. His idea of a romantic date is a trip to the observatory. But instead of gazing into the starry sky, he wants to talk with the astronomer about the earth's rotation.

When the Christian woman is confronted with one of these types, she must immediately dissuade him from any hope of romantic involvement. If asked for a date, she should politely decline with some excuse about having to take care of her seven children and a doctor's appointment for treatment of her leprosy.

ROMANCE

Self expression is good; self-control is better.

ROMANCE

Praying On the First Date

When you were dating, do you remember the guy who always prayed on the first date he had with any girl?

At first you figured the young man must be extremely spiritual. Why else would he want to sit down before the evening began and ask for divine guidance and protection?

Then you went out with him, like a fool, only to realize his true motive was to hold your hand in a "saintly" grasp while he prayed ever-so-sincerely.

And you possibly could have excused his little game were it not for his desire later in the date to renew the first-century Christian practice of "greeting one another with a holy kiss."

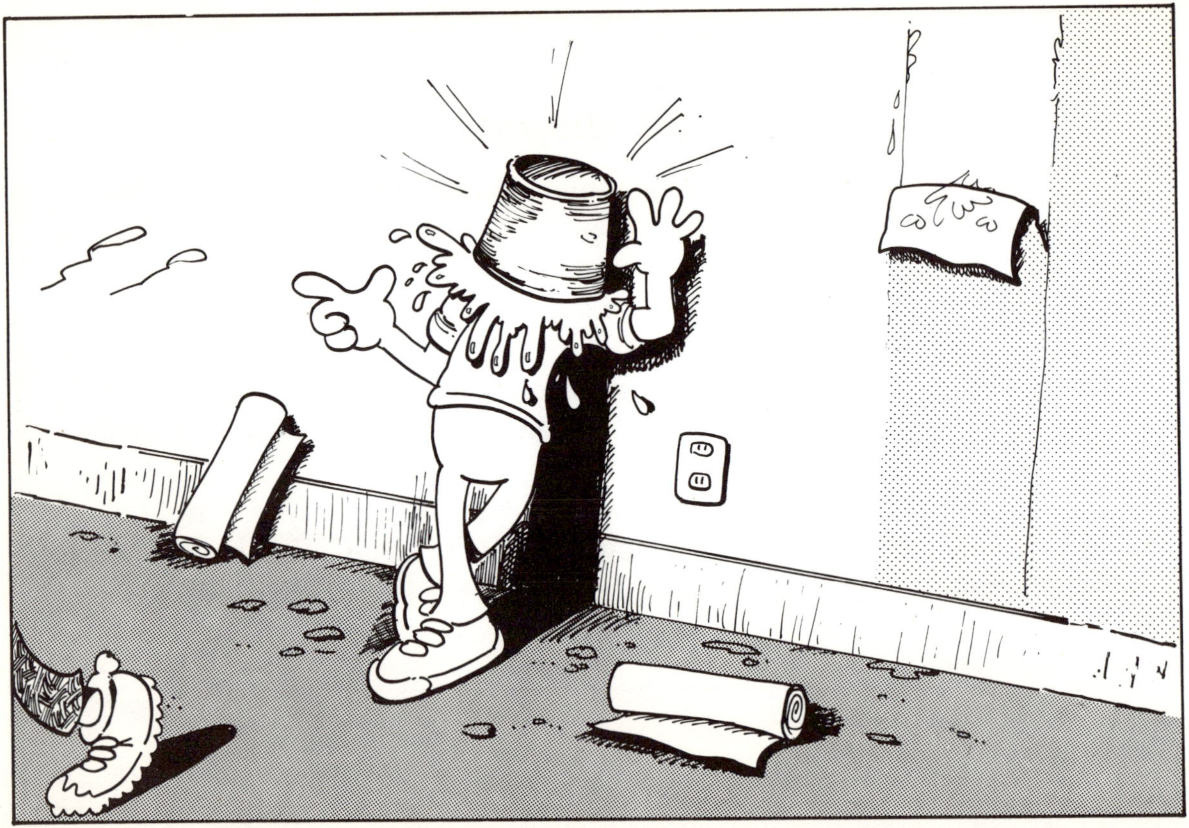

ROMANCE

Wallpaper

Experts tell us that the main problem in troubled marriages is a lack of communication. That may be high on the list, just above money and sex, but it's not number one. No, there's a home wrecker even more deadly than any of the above.

Wallpaper.

There's not another device, subject, or person on the face of this earth able to inflict pain or otherwise break up a harmonious relationship to a greater degree than wallpaper. Marriage counselors' offices are filled with couples who made the terrible mistake of attempting to select, cut, paste, and hang wallpaper...together.

Save your marriage. Paint the walls and put the money you will save into a weekend for two. Away from the kids. And away from the wallpaper.

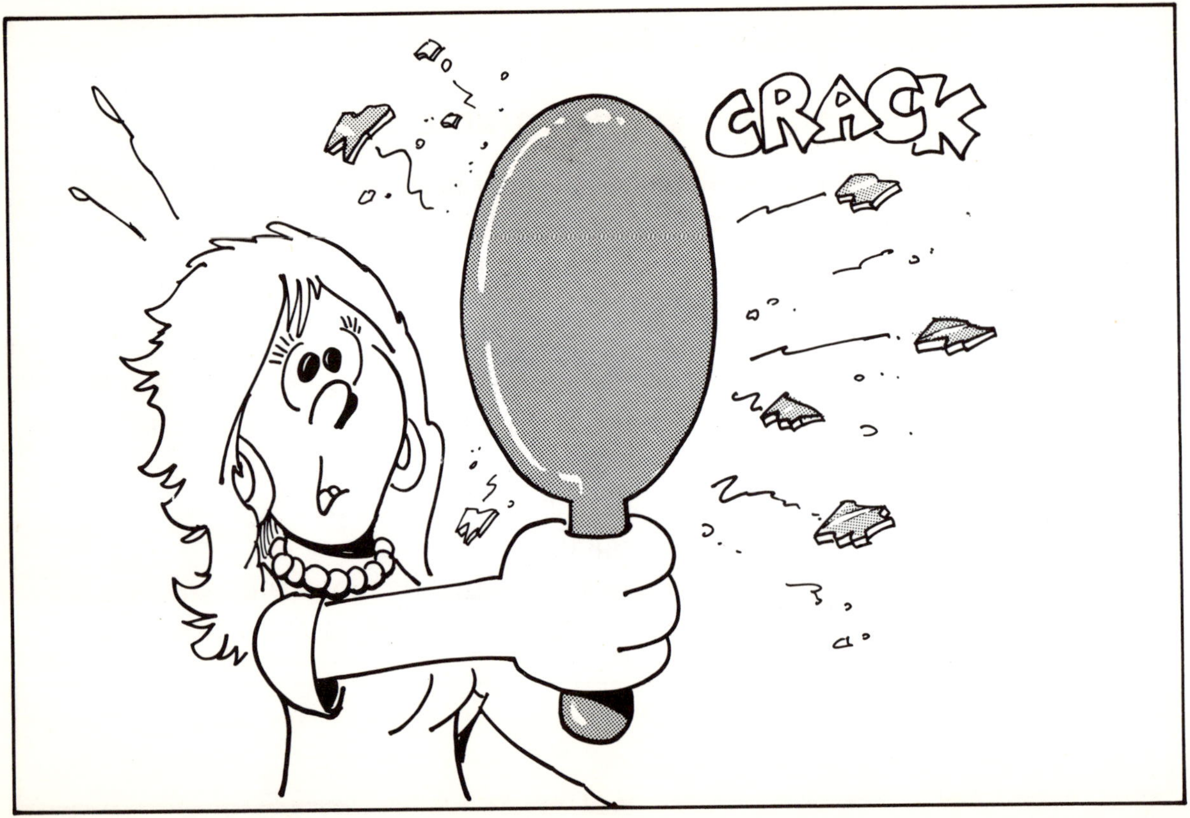
CRACK

ROMANCE

Always Look Your Best

Today's woman always strives to look her best. However, occasions may arise when time pressures and family demands will prevent her from following some of the basic rules of grooming and personal etiquette. Here are some guidelines women frequently forget:

1. **Never smile in a public place with boysenberry seeds stuck in your teeth.** This most commonly occurs after eating in a pie shop. Should you find yourself in this position and you feel you must smile, do so with your mouth closed.

2. **If you are sitting on a bus or a plane, and the person next to you asks permission to light a cigarette, kindly but firmly say no.** A proper response would be something like, "Go right ahead, it won't bother me. I already have cancer."

ROMANCE

3. ***Never tuck your dress into the back part of your underwear.*** This can occur after using the restroom during a break at work. The telltale sign that you have made this personal grooming error will be the snickers of your fellow office workers as you make your way back to your desk. Another give-away will be the draft on the back of your legs.

ROMANCE

There's a face-lift you can perform yourself that is guaranteed to improve your appearance. It is called a smile.

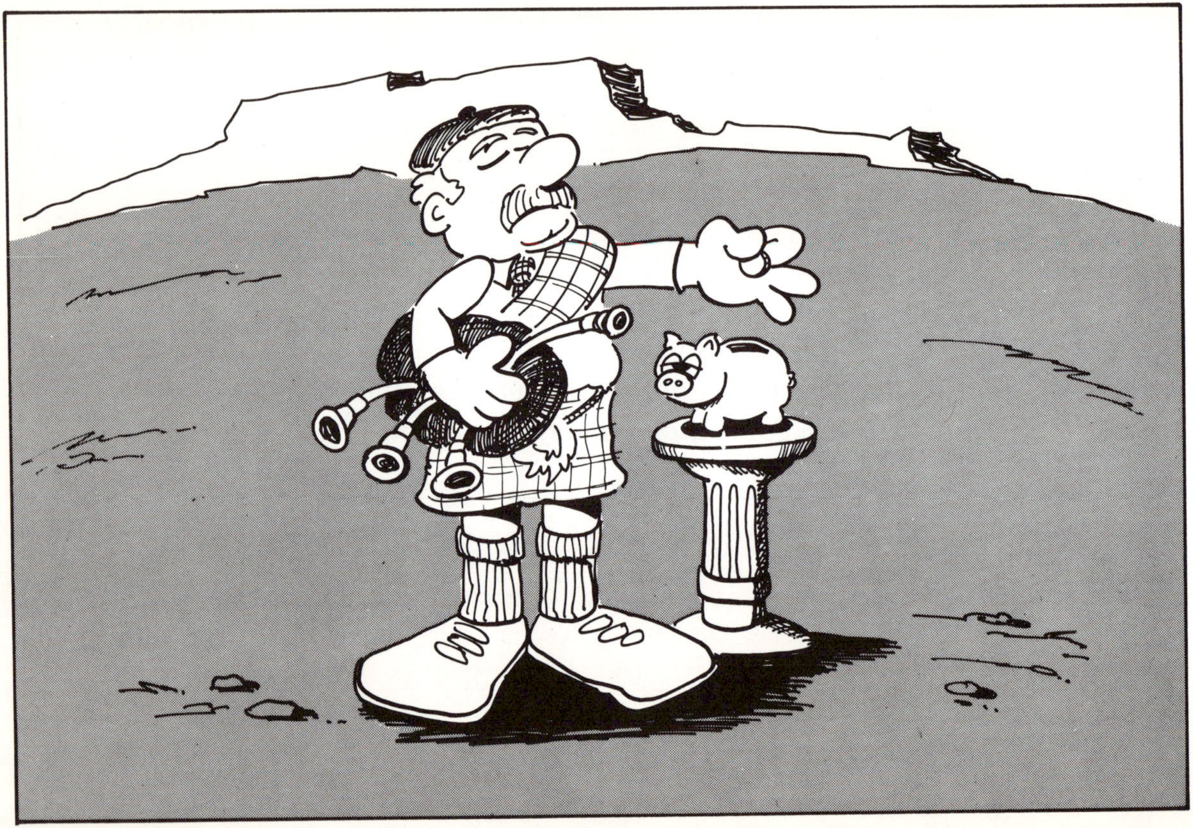

ROMANCE

The Wedding Anniversary

There is a special place in a woman's heart for her wedding anniversary. For most husbands, however, the event is about as significant as the street sweeper's annual trip by your house. Consequently, there is quite a contrast between how the wife would like to celebrate the occasion and how it actually turns out.

She *imagines* that he will send her roses in the afternoon with an invitation for a romantic dinner date that evening. In *reality,* he calls at 5:00 P.M. to say that he has to work late and asks if she has picked up his bowling shirt from the cleaners.

In her *fantasy,* she sees him dressed in formal attire as he gallantly escorts her to a waiting limousine. In *reality,* he comes home from work hot and sweaty; then he changes into his "comfortable clothes"—his old pair of high school gym shorts with his last name stenciled across the rear, a pair of thongs, and a Dallas Cowboys T-shirt which has

ROMANCE

mustard stains down the front. Instead of escorting her to a limousine, he is sitting in their 1974 Plymouth Valiant (with a cracked windshield and no muffler) and is honking the horn for her to hurry up and get in the car.

She *envisions* a candlelight dinner in a French restaurant. With violin music in the background, he would romantically describe how he loves her. In *reality*, as close as she gets to a French dinner is the side order of French fries at McDonalds. And about the only romantic thing he does is arrange the Chicken McNuggets in the shape of a heart.

Her *fantasy* concludes with him taking her for a moonlit stroll and offering a beautifully wrapped gift to her in which she finds an expensive bottle of the perfume she has been wanting. What *actually* happens is about as close to her fantasy as she will ever come. During a television commercial, he tosses her a gift. Instead of being wrapped,

ROMANCE

it is still in the shopping bag with the sales receipt stapled to it. But inside the bag is exactly the kind of perfume she was hoping for.

How could he have known? He must have seen the Macy's ad which she clipped out and nonchalantly taped to his shaving mirror.

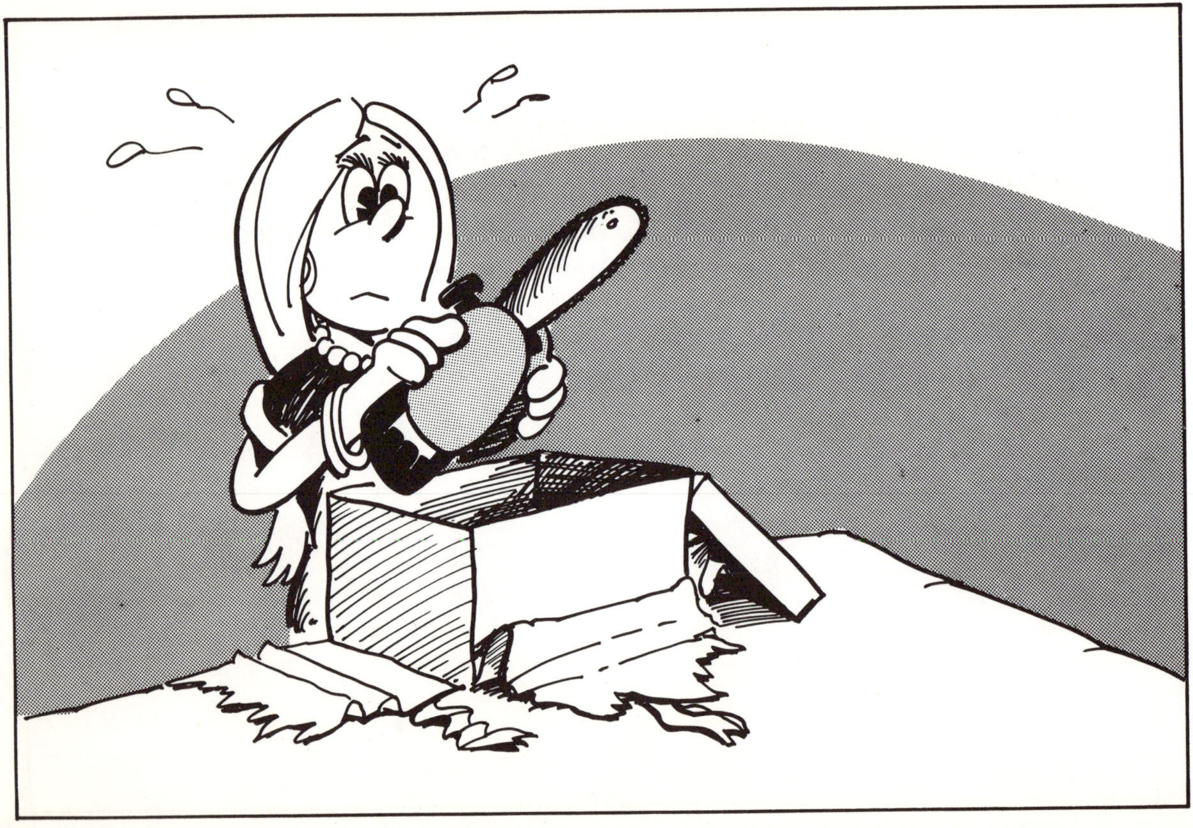

ROMANCE

You Know Your Love Life Is In Trouble When:

★   Your husband stops calling you his "Little Chickadee" and now refers to you as his "Dumb Cluck."

★   The anniversary gifts from your husband all come from the automotive department at Sears.

★   You stop wearing skimpy nighties on cold winter evenings because you prefer to sleep warmly in your parka and sweat pants.

★   A candlelight dinner-for-two happens only when the electricity goes out and you split a can of tuna with the cat.

★   Instead of flowers and candy on Valentine's Day, now all you get is a note of "I love you" scribbled across an FTD florist ad that has been cut out of the newspaper.

ROMANCE

★   The most romantic movie you have seen in the last five years is a rerun of **Son of Flubber.**

★   The romantic get-away weekend is cancelled so you can save the money to buy new sprinkler heads for the lawn.

ROMANCE

*A worthy wife is her husband's joy and crown;
the other kind corrodes his strength and
tears down everything he does.*

Proverbs 12:4

4

WORKING

At Home, At the Office, And In Other Disaster Zones

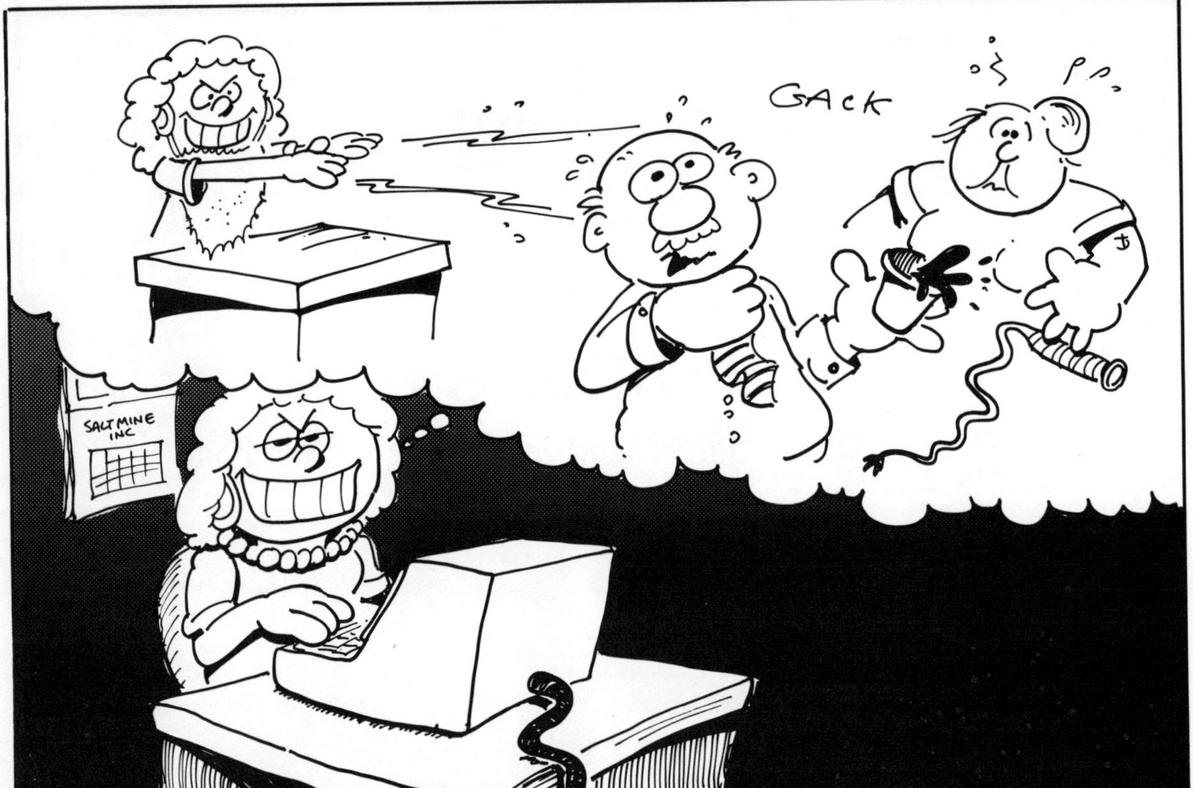
GACK
SALTMINE INC

Working

 Whether pushing pencils and pens from nine to five, or dealing with diapers and dustpans from dawn till dusk, you valiantly face the tasks which God has placed before you.
 In the office or at home, you strive at all times to do your best. Yet there are those times when you feel like an Israelite enslaved in Egypt. You fantasize about growing a Moses beard and casting the plague of boils on all those who are harassing you.
 The following illustrations are just a few of the indignities you are sometimes forced to endure.

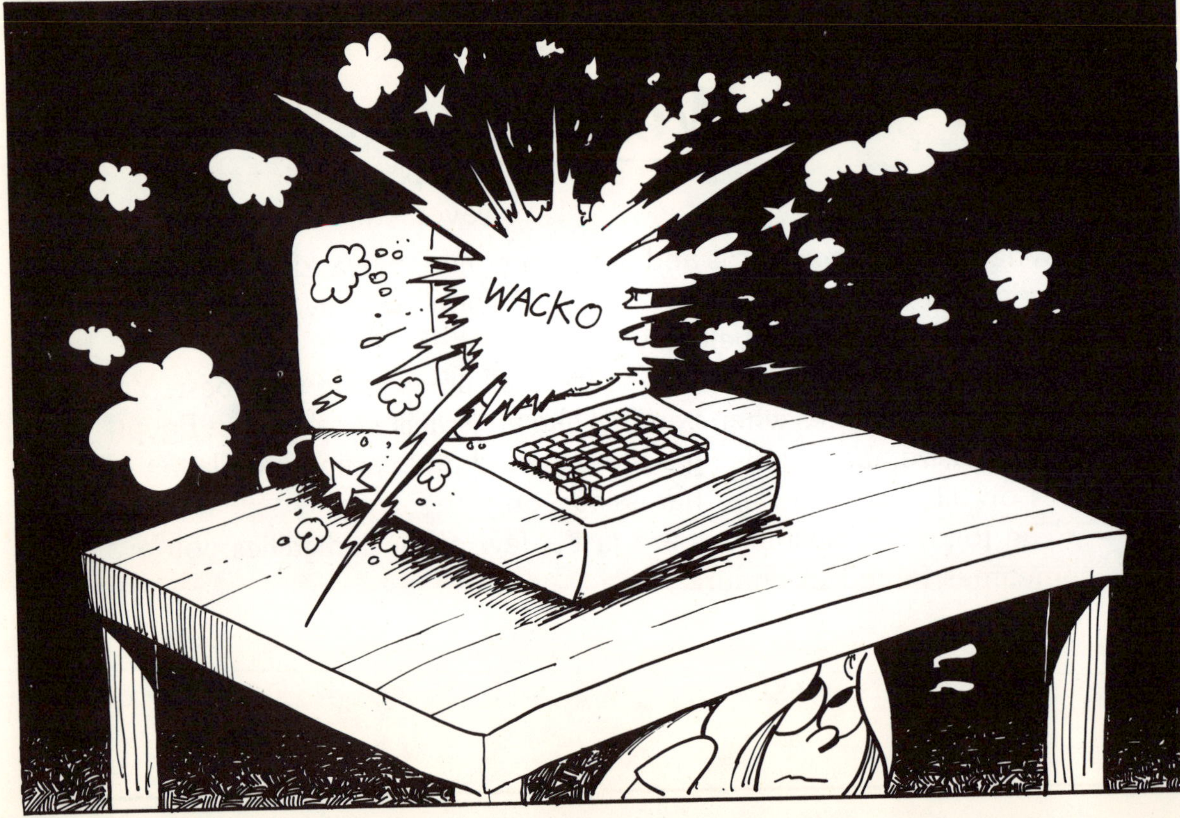
WACKO

Modern Times

Let's face it. Whether you like it or not, the space age is here, along with its vast array of computers, microwaves, satellites, and cable converters.

Perhaps you've been trying to hang onto the past by purchasing antique furniture and scattering Grandma's handmade doilies around the house. It just doesn't work. Modern times are creeping in.

Remember your first microwave oven? At last you could turn eggs into rubber or ignite aluminum foil with the push of a button.

Then there was your husband's first digital sports watch, an impressive gadget which required four hands to operate. Fortunately, the purchase price included a free seminar showing the two of you how to set it on daylight saving time.

Then there was the Christmas you gave your children a home video game system, the kind connected to your television so the kids can

WORKING

destroy planets, gobble up energizers, and ruin the picture tube.

Because the kids were now occupied after school, you decided to get a part-time job, something in the clerical field. Feeling confident in your high-school typing skills, you applied for a word processing position. Little did you know that meant sitting face-to-face with a "user friendly" computer.

It was friendly all right. But your new boss was anything but friendly, particularly after you somehow managed to tap into the company's private financial records.

At least you knew how to work the microwave oven in the staff eating lounge.

Grocery Shopping

Acquiring food for the family is an age-old task. It used to be the man's job to hunt down buffalo meat and grow potatoes for the family meal. But that was before the invention of the grocery store.

Since men are naturally allergic to shopping carts and plastic vegetable bags, it is now left to the woman to find the family food. Armed with little more than a crumpled shopping list, her Nike running shoes and a will to survive, a woman must pick her way through treacherous supermarket trails laden with culinary obstacles.

Her mind must operate with the precision of a computer as she decides whether three pints for a dollar is a better value than 58 ounces for $1.29. She must employ the skills of a diplomat as she tells the butcher his meat looks like it just came from the dog pound. And she must play the part of a psychologist as she tells her kids to calm down or be laid to rest in the frozen peas.

CHECK OUR PRICES!
DISCOUNT
PRODUCE
LOW LOW PRICES
SHOP AND COMPARE!
SALE

WORKING

It all comes to an end, of course, when the huntress finally gets her provisions home and into the cupboards, only to be told at breakfast the next morning: "Mom, you forgot to get a box of Fruit Flavored Captain Donutz cereal!"

If you can find a truly good wife, she is worth more than precious gems!... She gets up before dawn to prepare breakfast for her household, and plans the day's work for her servant girls.... She is energetic, a hard worker, and watches for bargains. She works far into the night!

Proverbs 31:10,15,17

WORKING

The Stay-At-Home Woman

In this day and age of the liberated woman, it's nice to know there are still people out there who think working at home as a full-time wife and mother is a noble calling. And why not? The fact of the matter is that the stay-at-home woman does more than cook, clean, and car pool. Indeed, she contributes to the overall health, education, and welfare of our country. For example:

Health—Moms and wives contribute to the all-important area of health science. Who do you think pushed nutritionists to the brink at General Junk Food until they finally came up with wholesome new delights like Liquid Waffles, Sugar Free Ding Dongs, and Freeze Dried Spam Casserole?

Education—Wives and mothers have always taken a personal interest in our nation's education. Who else would have come up with the idea of teaching kids the alphabet by putting magnetic letters on the refrigerator door? Who else could bake cookies and cupcakes for special school parties?

Welfare—Full-time moms and wives help keep America's work force on the job. Just think of how many game show hosts and soap opera actors would be out of work if it weren't for women watching daytime television.

There's no doubt about it. The full-time wife and mother is an invaluable commodity. Without her, our nation might very well fall apart.

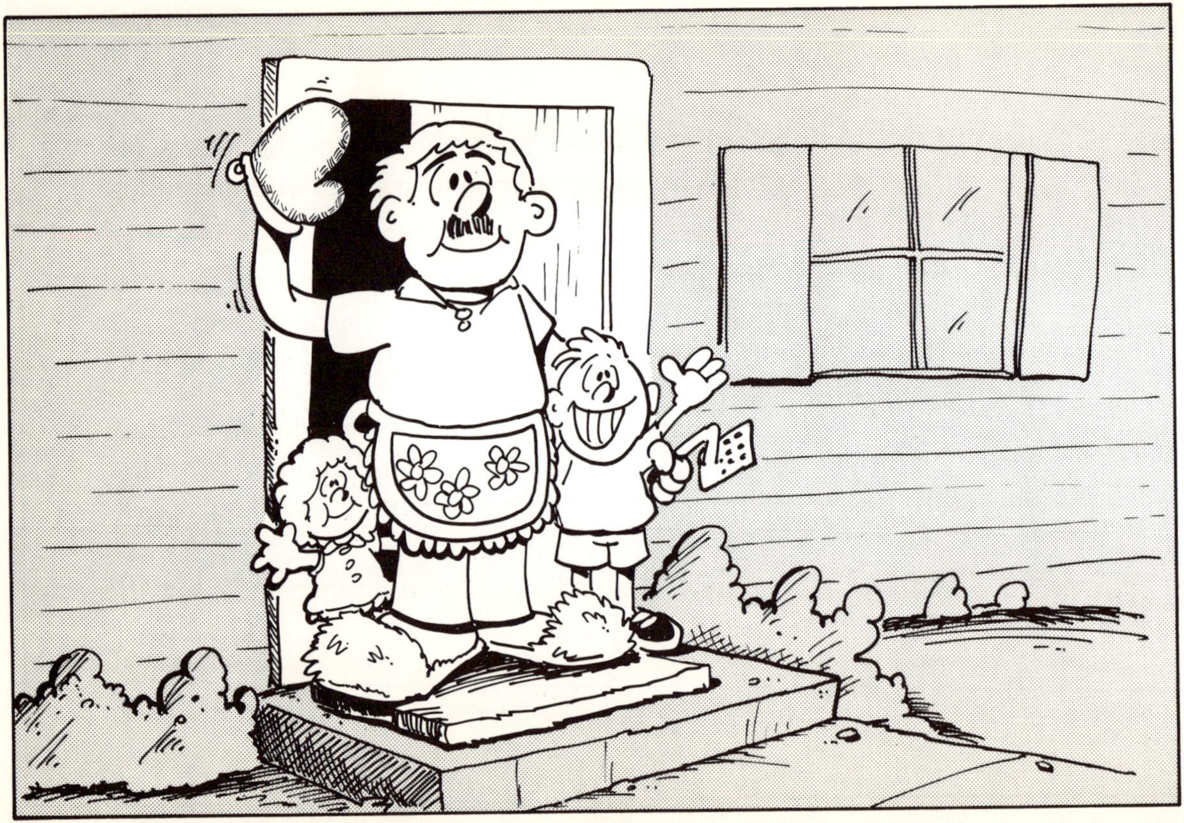

Mothering Husbands

The phenomenon of the working mother has produced a number of interesting side effects. There is, of course, the additional income for the family, the feelings of accomplishment and professional fulfillment, as well as the exposure to new technologies.

All of these, however, may be insignificant when compared to the effect your job has on your husband. Take a look at him. Notice the not-so-subtle changes. Is he helping more around the house? Is he taking out the garbage on the second request rather than the fourth? Does he take the kids to the doughnut shop on Saturday mornings now?

If so, then your spouse is becoming a part of the movement known as the "Mothering Husband." This movement started out innocently enough as the "shared household responsibilities" trend. It was a good trend, but has it gone too far? At first husbands were reluctant to do "women's work." Now they've not only become accustomed to it,

WORKING

but they actually enjoy playing the role you used to have.

If you don't believe it, give yourself the "Mothering Husband" test:

1. When you get home from work, do you find your husband juggling hot pads while wearing your gingham kitchen apron?
2. Has your husband contributed a recipe to the church cookbook within the last three months?
3. Do your kids actually have fun with their dad?
4. When you go to the State Fair, does your husband stop and stare open-mouthed at the salesman giving the Veg-a-matic demonstration?
5. Has your husband suddenly taken an interest in watching the public television channel with you?

WORKING

6. Does your husband refuse your romantic advances at times, claiming he has a headache?

If you answered "yes" to five of these questions, then you are married to a mothering husband.

Just about the time a woman's work is done for the day, her husband asks her to help him with the dishes.

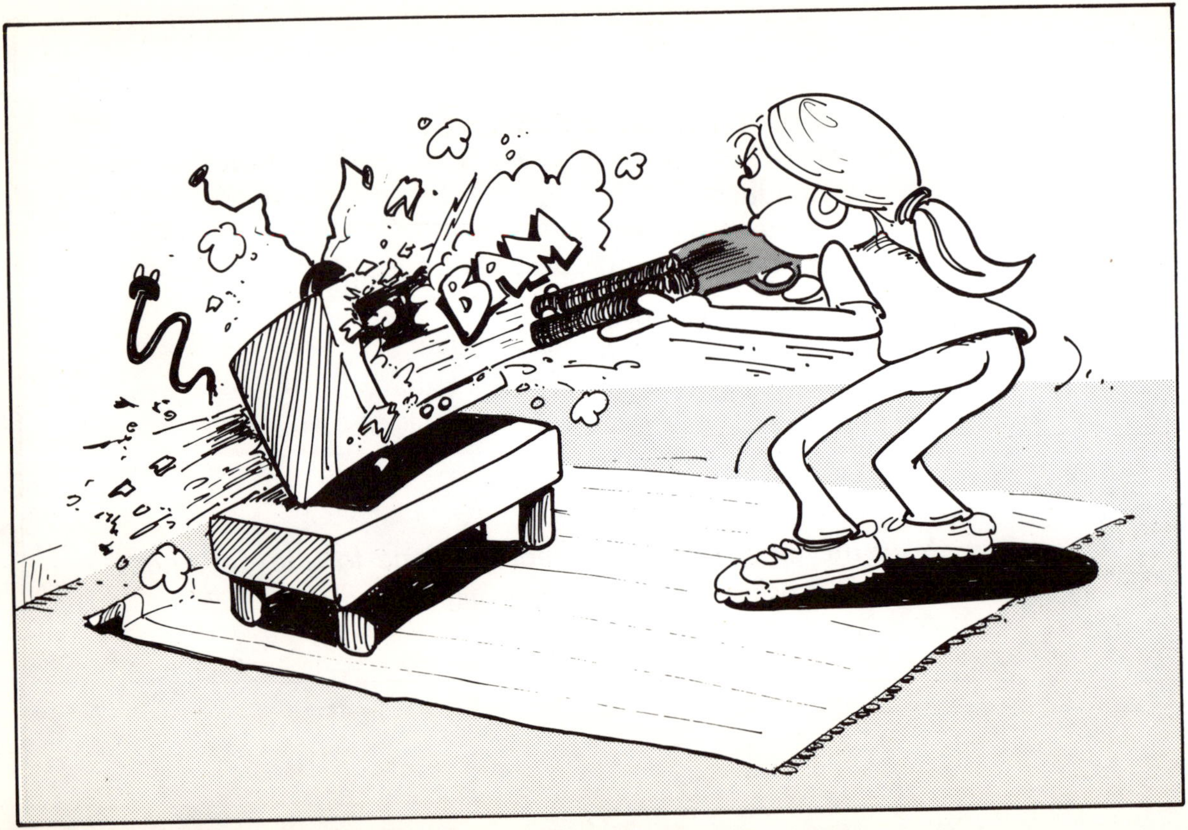
BAM

Women in Prime-Time

A woman's greatest enemy is the television. Over the years, television has given an **unrealistic** portrayal of women.

Take, for instance, the totally unrealistic "I Love Lucy" shows. How many women do you know who will dress up like a palm tree, ride the subway, and then try to sneak into her husband's nightclub to sing "Babaloo"?

The other extreme is the demure and meek behavior of June Cleaver. (You remember, the Beaver's mom.) June was always dressed in a blue dotted-Swiss dress, with pearls and wrist-length gloves. And that was her outfit for cleaning the garage. No, come to think of it, we never saw June doing any housework. She made Wally and Beaver clean the garage, but she did bring them hot cocoa.

The current television shows are more contemporary, but they also fail to portray women realistically. These shows tell us that to be fulfilled, a woman must be a detective for the police squad. How

WORKING

unrealistic! Most women don't carry a .38 revolver in their dress.

If she isn't a cop, then the woman on television is portrayed as some kind of Super Homemaker. She is either a business executive or a graduate student working on her doctoral thesis on ancient Tibetan architecture. At the same time she manages to raise her own three children plus two orphans. She is a coach for her son's soccer team, and she is considering running for governor.

Beyond all this, there is a segment in each episode of the television show which spotlights her use of psychology with her husband. The husband is always portrayed as some stubborn but well-intentioned chauvinist. She must overindulge him with flattery and attention. He is constantly making mistakes in everything from reading a map to disciplining the children. Then she must correct his mistakes and undo all the damage he has done without hurting his frail ego.

Come to think of it, maybe these television shows *are* realistic.

WORKING

*Work hard so God can say to you, "Well done."
Be a good workman, one who does not need to be
ashamed when God examines your work.
Know what his Word says and means.*

2 Timothy 2:15

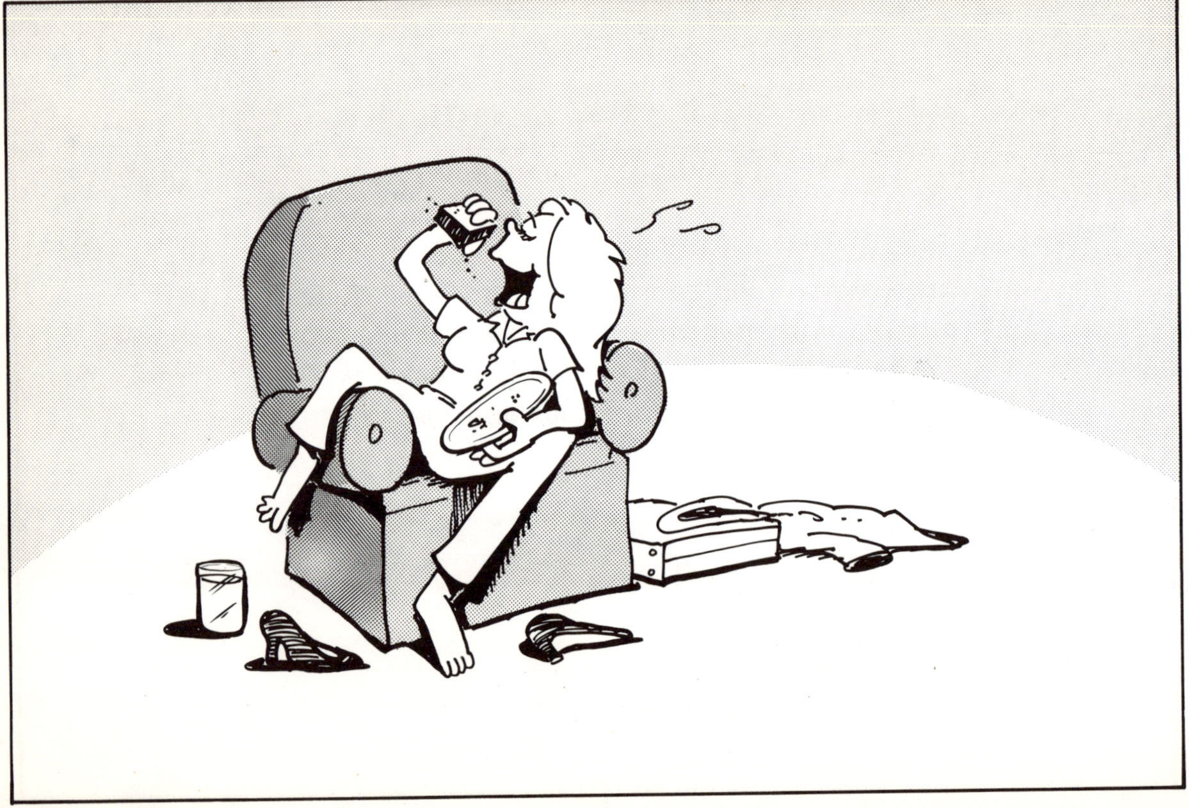

WORKING

You Know You've Had A Rough Day When:

★ You drive into the repair shop, and your mechanic starts singing: "I'm In The Money."

★ The deduction from the raise you just got is so big that you have to take a second job to replace the money you lost.

★ You tell the sales clerk you are looking for a pot holder and she directs you to the girdle department.

★ You are contemplating lining the rim of your boss's coffee cup with Super Glue.

★ You can't avoid the speeding ticket by flirting or crying because the police officer is a woman.

★ You eat an entire batch of brownies because you feel that you "deserve it."

★ After you drive home from work you rip the "Have a Happy Day" bumper sticker off your car.

5

GROWING OLDER
Can You Fool All of the People All of the Time?

*Seventy years are given us! And some may even live to eighty.
But even the best of these years are often emptiness
and pain; soon they disappear, and we are gone.
Teach us to number our days and
recognize how few they are;
help us to spend them as we should.*

Psalm 90:10,12

Growing Older Gracefully

Whether you are still in your tender twenties or have reached the status of "senior saint," you are probably more than a little concerned with the agonies of aging. You know that beauty is only skin deep, but your skin is what everybody sees. Thus, while you place a priority on developing your inward beauty which is important to God, you also attend to repairing and remodeling your external appearance so you won't be classified as a public eyesore.

With the Christian perspective which is uniquely yours, you will grow old gracefully, confident in the fact that there must be at least one other person who is falling apart faster than you.

Contrary to the literature which tells you how to stay young, the final words of **this** book will help you face up to the fact that your face is falling down.

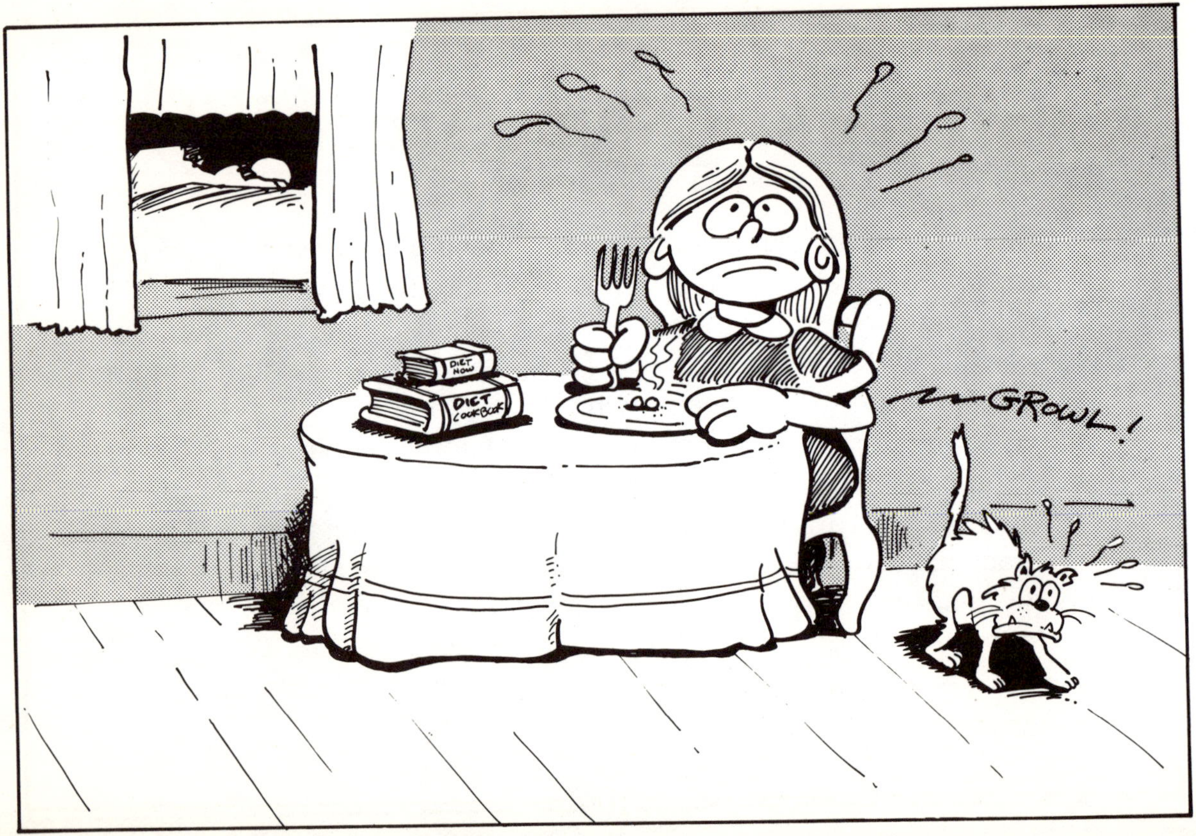
DIET NOW
DIET COOKBOOK
GROWL!

Dieting

Dieting is a social phenomenon. You wouldn't diet if you were living alone in the Gobi Desert. (No matter how fat you were, you'd still look pretty good compared to a camel.) Similarly, you probably wouldn't diet if all of your friends bought their dresses from the racks marked "Chubette" or "Junior Plenty."

Unfortunately for you, however, your best friend has long, lean legs and a waistline the size of a napkin ring. If **she** gains ten pounds, nobody notices. If **you** gain ten pounds, your stomach keeps moving when you stop walking. And if you gain fifteen pounds, little kids sneak up behind you and make elephant noises.

So you diet. First you try counting the calories of everything you eat. But this doesn't work because your calculator only has nine digits. Then you try those chocolate diet candies. But they taste so good you are reminded of the Hershey bars you hid in your panties drawer.

GROWING OLDER

Next, you order some of those guaranteed diet pills from the "All You Can Eat Diet" advertised in ***TV Guide***. After you have gorged yourself on cheesecake and Cheetos, you read the guarantee's fine print which says the diet pill is "all you can eat."

In desperation you try a liquid protein diet. Finally, you have some success, but three weeks without food leads you to do strange things: like hyperventilating in a bakery shop to sniff up all the aroma; or leaving nose prints and drool on the window of the See's Candy Store.

Life would be much easier if you had only fat friends.

GROWING OLDER

*Anyone who has ever gone on a diet knows which meal is the hardest one to skip—
the next one!*

GROWING OLDER

Say What You Like

One of the advantages of growing older is that you can say and do what you like and nobody seems to mind. You can be sarcastic, critical, or rude, and people think it's cute. Sometimes they even mistake your negative words for valuable advice.

"Take that dress off and put on something decent," you tell your 16-year-old granddaughter. "It looks like a dish towel someone wiped the floor with."

"This is home-baked bread?" you ask your daughter-in-law. "I thought you had put a hot pad on my plate by mistake."

"Thank you for the message, Reverend Filmore," you tell your pastor. "It gets better every time you give it. I can't wait until you get it right."

"The new blouse you gave me is lovely," you gush to your grandson ever so sweetly. "I hope you saved the receipt so I can return it tomorrow."

GROWING OLDER

Finally, at the annual family reunion, you delight in taking out your teeth and playing them like castanets to the tune of "Amazing Grace."

Don't talk so much. You keep putting your foot in your mouth. Be sensible and turn off the flow!
Proverbs 10:19

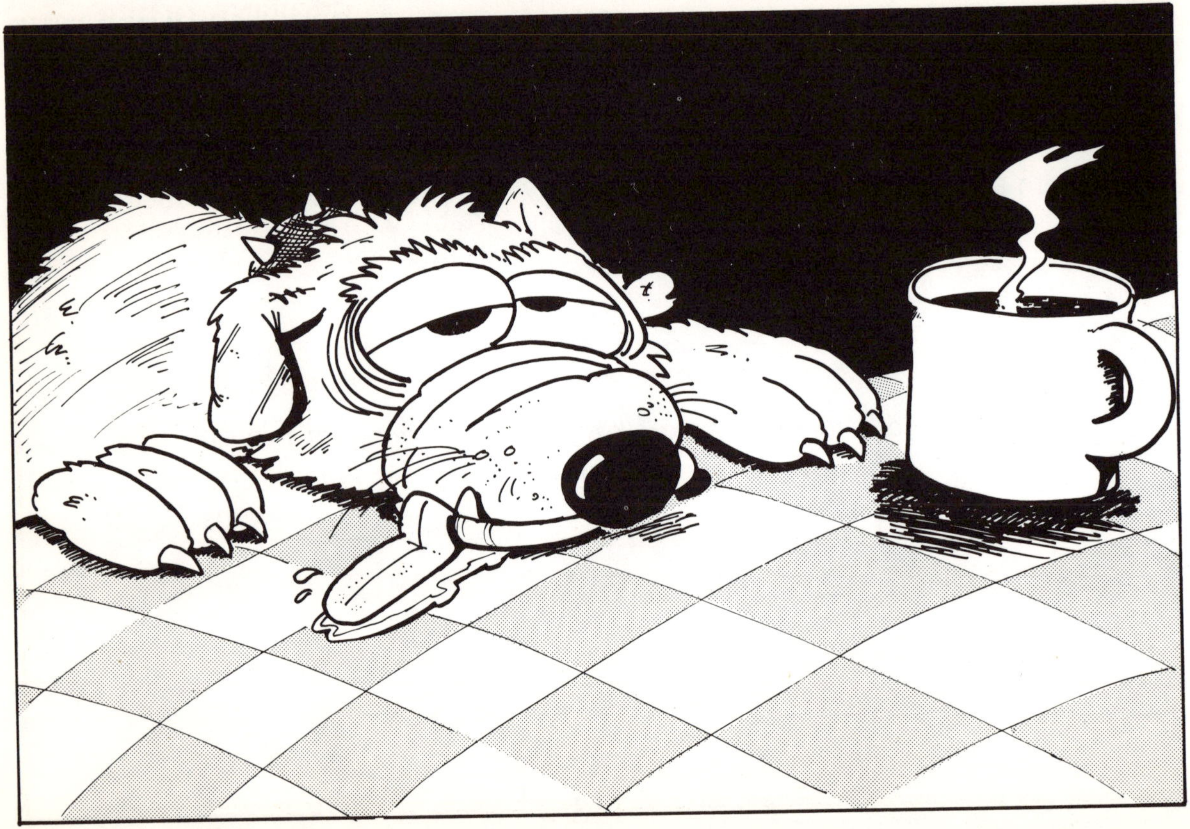

GROWING OLDER

The Family Dog

One sure sign of growing older is when the only living object in your house you can talk to and feel totally comfortable with is the family dog. This happens when the kids have gone off to college or gotten married, and you and your husband have your communication down to a series of grunts, winks, and scowls.

The family dog, on the other hand, is all ears. He's got nothing but time. And he loves you. Never mind that you're the only one who ever feeds him. He cares about you and wants to know how you feel. You can see the concern by looking in those big bloodshot eyes.

When you tell the family dog about your cares and concerns, he doesn't criticize you or top your problems with his. He just looks at you and yawns. You can make it, he tells you silently.

It's always a sad day when the old family dog dies. Suddenly there's just you and your husband, and it's not the same. His eyes are

GROWING OLDER

bloodshot, too, but they're not understanding enough. Never mind that you're the only one who feeds him. He doesn't seem to appreciate you the way your dog did.

Then by accident one day you pat your husband on the head and say, "Good boy." He looks at you rather longingly, and your instincts start to carry you along. You scratch behind his ears, stroke his back, and start telling him about your day. And he loves it!

Maybe there is life after Rover!

GROWING OLDER

Self-Improvement

As life begins to pass you by, you become painfully aware of what you have missed. You have never climbed the Swiss Alps; you have never taken an exotic ocean cruise; you have never even gone to the grocery store in a halter top.

So now is the time to probe all of life's adventures before you are too pooped to probe.

No more afternoons spent watching soap operas, eating chocolate bonbons, and gulping diet soda. Now your week is filled with French language classes, assertiveness training seminars, and piano lessons.

But alas. After four months you can only say two sentences in French: "I am in the street and do not have a chainsaw," and the very helpful phrase, "Waiter, please bring me the Eiffel Tower."

And after completing those lousy self-assertiveness seminars you are still shy. But not so shy that you won't ask for a refund.

GROWING OLDER

As for the piano lessons—well, let's just say that your idea of adventure does not include "Twinkle, Twinkle, Little Star" in a piano recital with ten other students, all of whom are six to eight years old (and who play better than you do).

So it is back to the television and the soap operas. But maybe your life can still have meaning. There is always the ***Guiness Book of World Records*** for "Most Bonbons Stuffed in a Mouth Without Choking."

GROWING OLDER

...I am bringing all my energies to bear on this one thing: Forgetting what lies ahead, I strain to reach the end of the race and receive the prize for which God is calling us up to heaven because of what Christ Jesus did for us.

Philippians 3:13-14

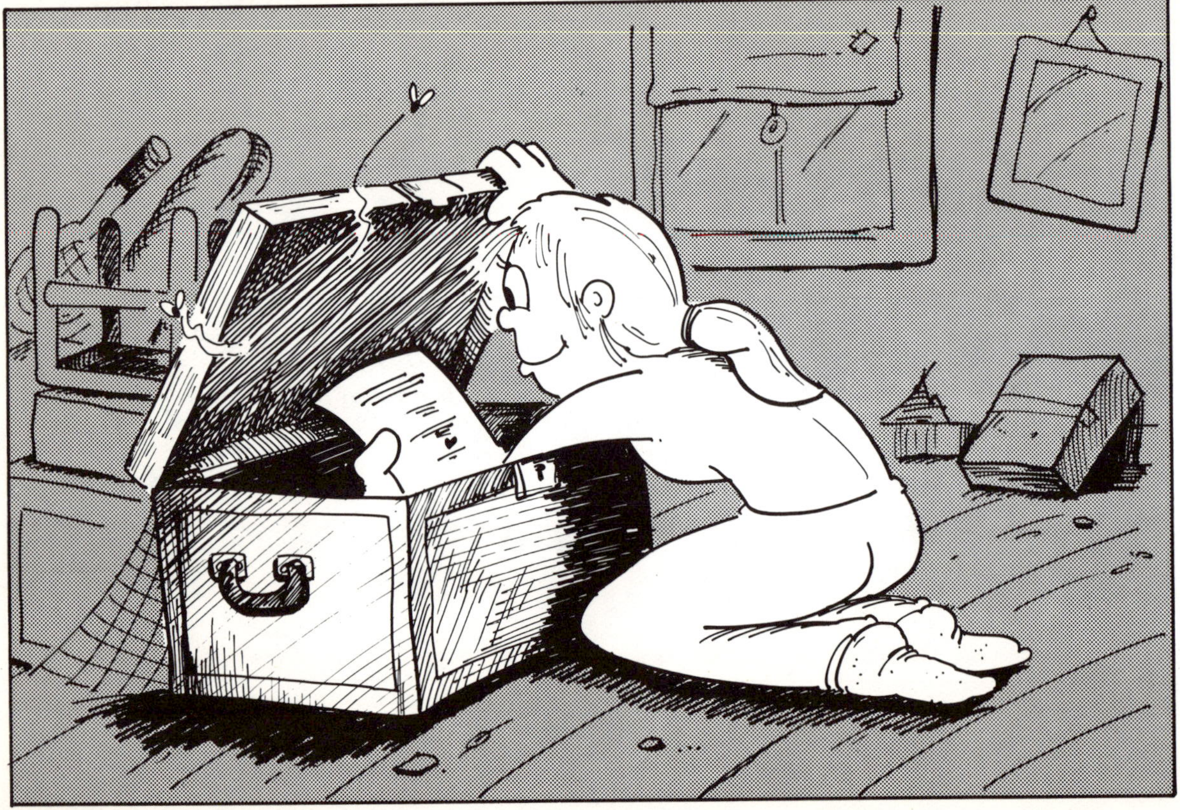

GROWING OLDER

Memories and Mementos

One of the pleasures of growing older is the occasional rummage through the trunk of mementos collected during your lifetime. There is a great feeling of joy as you recall those cherished moments. Looking at those old pictures and mementos brings to mind the special moments of your life, and you invariably wonder why you don't look in this trunk more often.

When you see your old high school yearbook, your mind immediately reflects on those days. You think about your friends and all the great times you had together. But then you also remember how embarrassed and humiliated you were that time they pinned a note to your back listing your name and telephone number and stating that you didn't have a date for the prom.

A few layers deeper in the trunk you find the wall hanging which your mother had placed in your bathroom. It was kind of a personal hygiene

GROWING OLDER

checklist she had embroidered when you were a little girl. It read: "Don't forget—toilet, teeth, face, hands, and nose." With some resentment you recall that your mother punished an omission of any of those items by giving you a double portion of lima beans at dinner.

Next you find a large stack of love letters written to you by your husband when you were dating him. Oh, how romantic he was then. He said such sweet and tender things. Hey! How come he never writes love notes to you anymore? And come to think of it, it's been a long time since you heard any sweet talk. The nicest thing he said in a month was when he complimented you on how well you cleaned out the garbage pail.

Another item you find is a sealed envelope. Inside are quite a few unflattering pictures of you at different ages. These are the "before" pictures that you took each time you started a diet. You had intended to take "after" snapshots to show how much weight you lost. But none

GROWING OLDER

of the diets lasted very long, and you never lost any weight.

Enough is enough! You don't mind the bad feelings toward your high school friends, your mother, or your husband. But this trip down Memory Lane is beginning to make you feel fat and guilty. So you throw all the junk back into the trunk and slam the lid shut. You run to the kitchen to get rid of your anger and frustration by eating an entire batch of raw cookie dough.

Now you know why you don't look in that trunk very often!

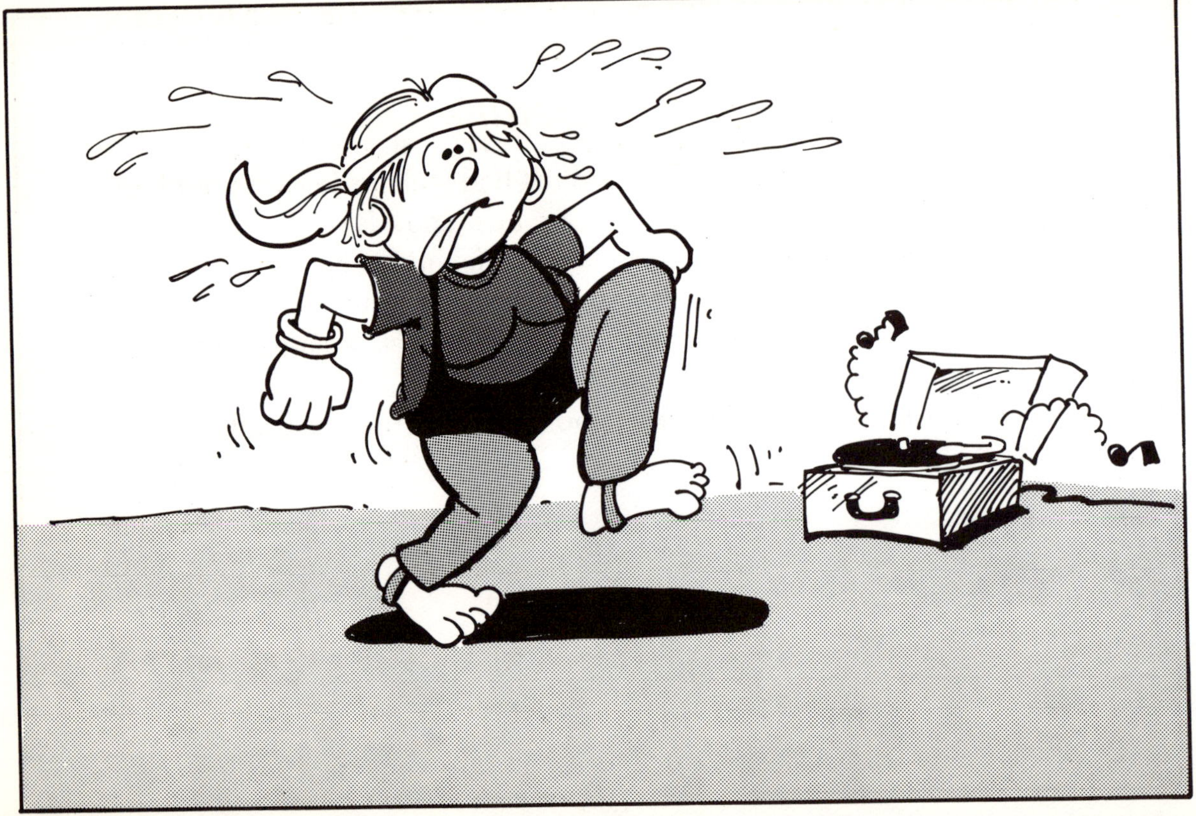

GROWING OLDER

You Know You Are Getting Older When:

★   You start wondering if any store carries industrial-strength deodorant.

★   You have to tuck in your belly button after every sneeze.

★   You have to turn your full-length mirror sideways to look at your hips.

★   You have to play the aerobics record at half-speed to keep up with the exercises.

★   You find this season's style of swimwear and bikinis to be vulgar, lewd, and disgusting mainly because when you put them on, your body looks vulgar, lewd, and disgusting.

★   You no longer refer to a woman who is your size as "fat," but instead call her a "full-figured woman."